BOOK ANALYSIS

By Luke Hilton

Infinite Jest
by David Foster Wallace

Shed new light
on your favorite books with

Bright
≡**Summaries**.com

www.brightsummaries.com

DAVID FOSTER WALLACE	**9**
INFINITE JEST	**13**
SUMMARY	**17**

- Tennis academy
- Big Indestructible Moron
- The entertainment
- The P.G.O.A.T.
- Quebecois separatists

CHARACTER STUDY	**25**

- Hal Incandenza
- Don Gately
- Orin Incandenza
- Mario Incandenza
- James Incandenza
- Avril Incandenza

ANALYSIS	**33**

- Addiction
- Mental illness
- Entertainment

FURTHER REFLECTION	**43**
FURTHER READING	**47**

DAVID FOSTER WALLACE

AMERICAN WRITER

- **Born in Ithaca, New York (USA) in 1962.**
- **Died in Claremont, California (USA) in 2008.**
- **Notable works:**
  - *Brief Interviews with Hideous Men* (1999), short story collection
  - *Consider the Lobster* (2005), essay collection
  - *The Pale King* (2011), unfinished novel

David Foster Wallace was a complex writer in terms of both his story-telling and the subjects and themes he explored. His work has influenced numerous contemporary writers and he is highly regarded for his work across the novel, short story and essay mediums. His work deals with diverse themes, including depression and mental illness, addiction, sport, entertainment and politics. His idiosyncratic writing style and expansive vocabulary make his fiction among the most instantly recognisable in modern literature.

Educated to a high level, Wallace published his first novel while still at college.

His works are often intimidating in their length and the detail Wallace gives the reader, but they are as funny as they are insightful. Indeed, one of the key characteristics of Wallace's writing was its ability to find humour in very dark situations. He was the recipient of a MacArthur Fellowship (commonly known as the MacArthur Genius Grant) and was a regionally recognised junior tennis player. This diverse biography reveals the wide sources from which Wallace found inspiration for his fiction. After suffering for most of his adult life with mental health problems, Wallace killed himself in 2008. He left the unfished manuscript for *The Pale King*, which was published posthumously to much acclaim. *The End of the Tour* (2015), a film starring Jason Segel as Wallace, was made based on David Lipsky's book detailing their time spent together on Wallace's *Infinite Jest* book tour.

INFINITE JEST

A NOVEL OF IDEAS

- **Genre:** novel
- **Reference edition:** Wallace, D. (2012) *Infinite Jest*. London: Abacus.
- **1ˢᵗ edition:** 1996
- **Themes:** addiction, mental illness, creativity, talent, entertainment, drugs, politics

Infinite Jest is David Foster Wallace's magnum opus. It runs to over a thousand pages in paperback edition and includes almost 400 endnotes which are integral to the narrative structure and are sometimes many pages long themselves. Wallace deals with the contemporary condition of living in North America, exploring its neuroses and hidden dangers, as well as hypothesising on the future of such a world. The novel is full of details which are not relevant outside of the text, details which pertain to the fictional world Wallace has made, and this, coupled with the time it takes for many to read the novel, creates a completely immersive world.

The novel contains dozens of important characters and ideas but focuses primarily on Hal Incandenza, a prodigious tennis talent who lives and is educated at his parents' tennis academy in Boston, USA. Surrounded by so many similar talents, the novel explores the pressure to succeed that modern life can place on somebody and different choices that one can make to cope with these pressures. Hal's family are all given their own unique stories which explore other themes and ideas. *Infinite Jest*'s other protagonist is Don Gately, a recovering drug addict and former criminal who works in a drug and alcohol recovery house. The reader learns about his childhood and criminal youth in a complex story arc which intersects with the Incandenza's on numerous occasions. Despite the novel's intimidating size and reputation, it has sold over a million copies worldwide.

SUMMARY

TENNIS ACADEMY

Hal is a bright teenager, with excellent test scores and a bright future in "the Show" (professional tennis). Despite his savant-like ability with words, Hal has trouble feeling emotions, a problem he medicates with marijuana, which he smokes in secret in the tunnels and hidden places at the academy. His father, James Incandenza, killed himself when Hal was younger and Hal had never really felt connected with him, despite their abilities in tennis. He medicates with marijuana for the majority of the novel and occasionally watches entertainment cartridges his father (who was also a filmmaker) created. The academy has a number of gifted tennis players, many of whom are exceptional in academics as well. Mike Pemulis is Hal's closest friend and a trouble-maker. He is kept at the academy due to his mathematical abilities but lacks raw talent on the court.

A series of strange and inexplicable things occur throughout the academy, none stranger than a ghost or "wraith" which appears and moves objects around. The students at the tennis academy are not average school-age children: they deal with rigorous physical training and high-level academic tutoring, and still find time to play a nuclear fallout-themed game in their spare time. They are the type of teenagers who find global political warfare a fascinating way to spend their free time.

Aware that drugs testing is taking place, the students usually rely on Pemulis' ability to get clean urine to pass the tests, but Hal decides to quit his marijuana addiction. The novel's end comes in its first chapter (although at the time the reader is unaware that this is the end of the novel), in which Hal's speech becomes slurred during a college admissions interview, his face changes into a grotesque mask of itself and the interviewers look on in horror as Hal, who once found verbal communication the easiest thing in the world, becomes incapable of making sense.

BIG INDESTRUCTIBLE MORON

Don Gately is an enormous man with a poor upbringing. His mother was an alcoholic and this leads to Gately becoming dependent on alcohol, as he drank her alcohol to stop her from having too much. Because of his size and his relative lack of intelligence, other children he knew called him BIM, which stood for Big Indestructible Moron. His mother called him it as well, unaware of what it meant. Despite his brutish size, Gately is a friendly person who had the odds stacked against him. Eventually he becomes addicted to various types of drugs and falls in with a bad crowd. In order to fund his drug habit, he burgles houses. Through Gately and through other characters who go through the same things as Gately we learn about the horrors and indignity of addiction, but Wallace also shows how it is possible to remain trapped.

After a burglary in which a victim dies inadvertently, Gately faces prison but opts for drug rehab instead. He is well liked by the other residents and eventually takes on a job there once he is clean. The other residents rely on Gately and he eventually gets shot trying to protect one of them.

His injuries are severe and the last few parts of his story are confused and difficult as he tries to make sense of his unconscious life in the intensive care unit of a hospital where, against doctor's orders, he refuses any kind of narcotic pain medication. His story ends with waves breaking against a shore and the reader is unsure what has happened to him.

THE ENTERTAINMENT

James Incandenza did not only play junior tennis and run a tennis academy but, prior to his death, was also a relatively successful creator of film cartridges or "entertainments", as they are sometimes known in the novel. Much of his work was satirical and ironic, but came from his love of optics and cameras. His masterwork is the missing *Infinite Jest*, a film which is said to be so entertaining that it will kill you if you watch it, as you are unable to do anything *but* watch it once you have seen it. It kills a Saudi Arabian attaché during the course of the novel and is highly sought after for its properties as a weapon. Although for most people it is deadly, James created the entertainment in order to connect with his emotionally stunted son, Hal.

THE P.G.O.A.T.

Joelle van Dyne is also known as Madame Psychosis, as well as the P.G.O.A.T. (Prettiest Girl of All Time) by Orin Incandenza (Hal's brother). Her beauty is said to be astounding and she captures the attention of most of the male characters she meets. Not only is Orin (a very successful and popular sportsman) besotted with her, but so is James Incandenza, who uses her as a muse and actor in his entertainment cartridges. She presents an eerie radio show as Madame Psychosis where she gains the affection of many people using only her voice. She becomes addicted to crack cocaine, and after trying to kill herself goes to the drug recovery house with Don Gately. During this time she is wearing a veil and declares that she will never show her face again. Although the reader is unsure whether this is true or not, she reveals that the veil is to hide her disfigurement, caused by her jealous mother throwing acid in her face after her father admitted to being attracted to her.

QUEBECOIS SEPARATISTS

The novel itself is set in the near future, at a time when the years have been replaced with sponsors, so that a particular year will no longer be referred to with numbers but with a brand name (such as the Year of the Whopper). In this hypothetical future, the United States and Canada have joined with Mexico to form one large country, the Organisation of North American Nations (O.N.A.N.), but this is not appreciated by the Quebecois separatist groups, one of which is comprised solely of people in wheelchairs. Their various clandestine actions all revolve around finding a rumoured entertainment cartridge which has the potential to be used as a weapon to ensure that their demands for separation from O.N.A.N. are met. They use double agents and liaise with members of the O.N.A.N. government itself, and much of this subplot involves getting closer to the Incandenzas, as it is believed their father James created the cartridge.

CHARACTER STUDY

HAL INCANDENZA

Hal is the novel's protagonist and one of the characters through whom Wallace deals with many of the narrative's themes and messages. Hal's drug use presents an unusual portrait of addiction when compared with that of Don Gately and the other residents of the drug recovery house: he smokes marijuana and nothing stronger and does so in complete secrecy and isolation. Hal's drug use challenges perceptions of addiction in that he is an incredibly smart and erudite young man, with many talents and abilities. His addiction should be a contradiction, but the more we learn about his emotional troubles, the more it seems to make sense.

Hal's emotional troubles are a mystery, but possibly stem from a traumatic experience of ingesting some mould as a child, an event that is repeatedly referred to in the novel. He has friendships with the other students, and is brotherly with his eldest sibling Orin and kind and compassionate with his other older sibling Mario. Despite this, the drug use appears to be a way for Hal to cope with long-repressed feelings. He recounts tricking therapists into thinking he was cured using his intelligence and reveals the guilt he felt at his father's suicide. The final event of the novel, in which Hal's admissions interview goes horribly wrong, seems to represent a literal slipping of this mask. Although Hal cannot tell that anything bad is happening, the reactions he gets are: "Sweet mother of Christ" and "Good God" (p. 12). Although the reader cannot be sure what exactly has happened either, Hal's worst fears have become a reality and he has shown his true self to others.

In addition to the addiction suffered by Hal's character, Wallace uses him as a representation of what might happen when the pressure of success is placed on somebody at too young an age. The constant drive for excellence might be a contributing factor to Hal's addiction, his anhedonia (inability to feel pleasure), and his self-destructive behaviours.

DON GATELY

Gately is another contradictory character in Wallace's novel. He is large and potentially brutal, but also reasonably gentle and kind. Despite the crimes he commits throughout the text, the reader feels sorry for him and wants the best for him. His childhood is revealed to be the main reason for his terrible adult life, and the strength he shows in order to become a functioning member of the recovery community demonstrates the quality of his character.

Gately's characterisation is as somebody who seems to keep finding himself in situations that he never really wanted to be in, and often does not understand how he gets there when he does. He is a fervent believer in the 12-step recovery programme but simultaneously finds it impossible to imagine a higher power to put faith in (as one of the steps dictates). He also finds that no matter what he tries, despite being able to give up the severely debilitating drugs he was on, he has never been able to give up cigarettes (or "gaspers", as he calls them). This sort of thing is typical for somebody as humble and self-deprecating as Gately. He regularly talks about himself as somebody who is inferior in intelligence.

The tragedy of Gately's character is in the things that have happened to him, and the way in which his response to them seemed to be the only one available to him. His mother's cigarettes, like her alcohol, were the first he ever tried, and despite his passion for high-school football, after that exposure to substances so early in life "he never played organized ball again" (p. 906). Similarly, his final act is one of desperation. After taking a bullet for a member of the recovery house he is taken to the ICU, where narcotic painkillers are the obvious solution, but he desperately wants to avoid that. It is as if he knows that if his pain is killed then his sobriety will be over; for Gately, there is not a positive choice to make.

ORIN INCANDENZA

Orin is Hal's oldest brother and a successful American football player. He was the one-time boyfriend of Joelle van Dyne, the 'Prettiest Girl of All Time', and now lives in Phoenix, where he sleeps with dozens and dozens of women without becoming emotionally attached to any of them. He speaks with Hal occasionally and never with any of the other members of his family, with whom he has a strained relationship. His relationship with his mother is strange, and this manifests itself in Orin's preference for sexual partners who are mothers. He refers to the women he sleeps with as his 'subjects'.

MARIO INCANDENZA

Mario is the middle child of the Incandenza family and shares a room with Hal at the tennis academy. He was born prematurely and suffers from various disabilities which stop him from reaching the same sporting and academic heights as his siblings. Despite this, Mario is never bitter or annoyed, but instead is a kind and caring individual and has no bad words to say about anybody. He makes amateur films which are often a big hit with the other residents of the tennis academy. Although popular and well liked, Mario is never really close with anybody outside of his family, as if the difficulties he faces put others off him.

JAMES INCANDENZA

James is the head of the family and is deceased throughout much of the novel, having died by suicide before the events of the narrative commence. The reader is slowly introduced to the idea that the ghostly "wraith" that is seen throughout the tennis academy and by Don Gately in the ICU is James' apparition. While alive, James was a filmmaker who drank to excess. His favourite drink was Wild Turkey (a strong bourbon whiskey) and he is regarded as an alcoholic. We are given glimpses into James' childhood, in which his own father drunkenly made him practice tennis over and over again. The difficulty of being pressured into this role by his father while having a greater interest in optics and filmmaking provides insight into Wallace's desire to understand the reasons behind addiction. His films are often difficult and strange, making fun of the craft or the critics, and yet he was able to complete a film such as the eponymous Infinite Jest which has extraordinary power. His death and his inability to communicate with his youngest son Hal are two of the underlying themes of the novel. His death (by microwaving his own head) leads Hal to enter the house and hungrily wonder what smells so good, in an example of Wallace injecting black humour into a very dark situation.

AVRIL INCANDENZA

Avril is the mother of the Incandenza boys and James' wife, who now runs the tennis academy with Charles Tavis. She is controlling and obsessive, which seems to bother Orin more than any of the others. He kindness is often assumed to be an attempt at gaining control. She is Canadian and subject to suspicion of involvement in the novel's sub-plot of Quebecois separatism. Having had many affairs during James' lifetime, including possibly conceiving Mario with Charles Tavis, she eventually has an affair with another Canadian: John Wayne, an underage tennis prodigy at the academy.

ANALYSIS

ADDICTION

Infinite Jest is a novel of addiction as much as it is a novel of anything else. Each of the major character suffers with some form of addiction, either to alcohol, drugs, control or sex. Wallace himself is rumoured to have battled with addictions in his life and the novel seems to reflect a sincere acknowledgement of the reality of facing such a contradictory and painful life. In the case of his characters, however, these contradictions are what give the narrative so much power and force. Adam Kelly writes that "Don Gately commits to praying to a Higher Power of which he cannot conceive, but which mysteriously enables his recovery" (Kelly, 2014: 3). This contradiction is both humorous and reflects the stark reality of addiction. For Gately, and many of the other characters, their addiction is something that they cannot fully comprehend. It goes beyond their understanding, and so it follows that Gately might find himself cured of it through accepting something that he also cannot understand. In presenting the character this way, Wallace suggests not that religion is a helpful tool exactly, but that it is clear how addicts find it to be so.

Wallace shows that these contradictions are commonplace. His descriptions of Hal explore how somebody who seems to have things together can be so utterly lost:

> "Like most young people genetically hard-wired for a secret drug problem, Hal Incandenza also has severe compulsion-issues around nicotine and sugar. Because smoking will simply kill you during drills…" (p. 395)

The fact that Wallace highlights that Hal's problem is not unique and is actually shared by many young people who have secret drug problems might appear as a joke, but it is a sincere way of exploring the nature of addiction, in that it can strike anybody at any time. His implication is that there is something within Hal that makes him more susceptible to these drug problems, but he also implies that it is not a particularly rare problem, since the behavioural side effects are known. Hal's contradictoriness in his addiction is shown by his need for nicotine but unwillingness to smoke since it hurts his tennis playing, despite the obvious fact that smoking marijuana will end his tennis career if picked up in a drugs test.

The way in which these contradictions keep coming to the fore of *Infinite Jest* illustrates the difficulty of the problem itself. Hal's extreme anxiety and paranoia are partly caused by his addiction, but at the same time his drug use is the only thing that can relieve them. Gately's crude and violent behaviour as a burglar is nothing like his sober self, and yet he wilfully committed these crimes in order to feed a habit that would only lead to more crimes. The novel contains countless other examples from drug users and alcoholics, as well as Orin, who takes no pleasure in the sex to which he is addicted. Although the constant darkness in these stories might appear bleak, it is balanced with a dark humour that becomes funnier the longer you spend reading about the characters. The fact that Wallace gives each of his characters a self-destructive addiction speaks to how he sees the world. His characters imply that nobody is perfect and that everybody is more than capable of damaging themselves due to the pressures of society and family.

MENTAL ILLNESS

The theme of mental illness is closely connected with addiction in *Infinite Jest*. Although Wallace does not specifically say that one leads to the other, they are connected more often than not. Just as each character battles with their own addictions, so too do they deal with mental health problems. Hal's paranoia and emptiness is a mental health problem that he ultimately succumbs to: after attempting to self-medicate and then to withdraw, he experiences a breakdown at his admissions interview. Once again, it is the contradictions in the characters that reveal the mental illnesses they suffer with. Kelly writes that "Wallace's self-conscious characters [are] shown to be prone to internal division and constantly engaged in dialogue with themselves and with others" (Kelly, 2014: 7). But as with Hal, much of the dialogue they have is superficial and lacking in any real weight, and despite being, like many of Wallace's characters "desperate for genuine reciprocal dialogue" (*ibid*.), he never finds a way of connecting with anybody on a deeper level.

Wallace repeatedly connects the theme of mental illness to the ills of society itself. Through resident of the recovery house Kate Gompert, he explores the different types of depression that people experience. He suggests that *"anhedonia or simple melancholy"* (p. 692) is a more common affliction consistent with the "what-does-it-all-mean-type crisis of middle-aged Americans" (p. 693) and that it is "not overtly painful" but is "disconcerting and… well, depressing" (*ibid*.). Wallace implies that this kind of mental illness is societally driven and afflicts people who do not meet their goals and expectations in life, and that this is why many of the academy's residents believe James Incandenza's suicide was a result of this (as he was a goal-oriented person). Of the tennis academy students, he says that they believe "the continent's second-ranked fourteen-year-old feels exactly twice as worthwhile as the continent's #4" (*ibid*.), which implies a belief about success and goals that is causing mental illness through its simple un-achievability. Wallace compiles an encyclopaedia of knowledge and anecdotes about mental illness into *Infinite Jest*, much of which places the blame squarely on circumstances which are out of his characters' control. Just as with *simply melancholy*, he suggests there is another form of depression, a "Great White Shark of pain" (p. 695), which is "a level of psychic pain wholly incompatible with human life" (*ibid.*).

Wallace's take on mental health seems to suggest that it is a universal (or at least American) phenomenon that is experienced by everybody at some point or another to different degrees of severity. Hal theorises that people are afraid of "being really human, since to be really human (at least as he conceptualizes it) is probably to be unavoidably sentimental and naïve and goo-prone and generally pathetic" (p. 695). The idea is that a fear of being human must originate in societal expectations and norms, which again implies that the mental illnesses that are suffered by people in fiction and in real life might be aided by honest and clear communication, and made worse through the fear of exposure.

ENTERTAINMENT

Entertainment is a central theme of *Infinite Jest* and a way in which Wallace deals with the themes of mental illness and addiction. The slightly futuristic setting of the novel means that the characters do not speak of VHS or DVD but of entertainment cartridges, many of which are made by James Incandenza and kept in a viewing room at the tennis academy. The deadly film is often referred to simply as *the* Entertainment.

An obvious reading of the presence of this film in the novel is as a critique of the numbing effect that television and films might have on a person, that this deadly Entertainment has just taken that to its logical conclusion whereby entertainment becomes so entertaining that it overtakes the rest of a person's life, just like a drug addiction might. However, Wallace was a scholar of television and entertainment as much as a writer of fiction. Philip Sayers suggests that Wallace was in a predicament in writing this novel, whereby "some kind of balance must be achieved" between "entertainment, commercialism [and] art, demanding too much of the reader without sufficient reward" (Sayers, 2014: 110). Just like television, Wallace wanted his novel to be entertaining, but he also saw that there was an important element to entertainment where it was worth thinking about and working for meaning and interpretation. The fun in reading his novel is never undermined by the complexity of it. James Incandenza's deadly film might be a representation of what happens with entertainment when it becomes all about gratifying the audience rather than making them appreciate and engage in what they are seeing. "The torpor-inducing effect of the Entertainment is far more potent than that of the attaché's usual selection of cartridges" (Sayers, 2014: 108), and the watcher is induced into a sleep-like coma, similar to the experience of overdosing on hard drugs. Rather than comparing entertainment to drugs, Wallace seems to imply that they are similar, and can both be equally damaging when the object of obsession or addiction. If either are used in order to numb oneself to the world, then they will be habit-forming and exacerbate mental illness. Whether it is cocaine or entertainment cartridges, Wallace suggests that what a person consumes can just as easily consume them.

Although unavoidably dangerous, just like drugs, entertainment in Wallace's novel can have a redemptive feature: communication. This feature is explained by the ghost of James Incandenza as being the motive behind the deadly film.

> "To concoct something the gifted boy couldn't simply master and move on from to a new plateau. Something the boy would love enough to induce him to open his mouth and come out – even if it was only to ask for more" (p. 839)

His motives behind the last film he made before his death are to try and find a way to communicate with his son. Hal's emptiness and anhedonia, so believed James, could be overcome by a film so tremendously compelling that he would not be able to internalise it and move past it so swiftly, as he had done with all other aspects of his life. The emphasis put on the idea of coming out speaks to the devastating effect that internalising mental illness and addiction can have on people; they grow inwards instead of outwards and cease to be members of a society. All James wanted was a way to make his son engage with the world around him, and not to be lost in his head.

FURTHER REFLECTION

SOME QUESTIONS TO THINK ABOUT...

- What do you think is happening to Hal at the start/end of the novel?
- Which of the novel's many secondary characters has the most tragic story? Explain your answer.
- What do you think Wallace is saying with the sponsorship of the years?
- What do you think happens to Gately at the end of the novel?
- Do you think the novel is positive about the 12-step method of recovery? Why/why not?
- Find an example of humour being used in tragic circumstances? What are the effects of it?
- Besides drugs/alcohol/cigarettes, what other types of addiction are present in the novel?
- What is the effect of the endnotes on your reading experience?
- Do you think the political alliance that is the O.N.A.N. has positive qualities, or is it merely satirical?
- What do you think the novel has to say about success? Explain your answer.

*We want to hear from you!
Leave a comment on your online library
and share your favourite books on social media!*

FURTHER READING

REFERENCE EDITION

- Wallace, D. (2012) *Infinite Jest*. London: Abacus.

REFERENCE STUDIES

- Kelly, A. (2014) David Foster Wallace and the Novel of Ideas. In: Boswell, M. ed., *David Foster Wallace and "The Long Thing"*. London: Bloomsbury, pp. 3-22.
- Sayers, P. (2014) Representing Entertainment in *Infinite Jest*. In: Boswell, M. ed., *David Foster Wallace and "The Long Thing"*. London: Bloomsbury, pp. 107-126.

ADDITIONAL SOURCES

- Wallace, D. (1993) E Unibus Pluram: Television and U.S. Fiction. *Review of Contemporary Fiction*. 13(2), pp. 151-194.

Bright Summaries.com

More guides to rediscover your love of literature

www.brightsummaries.com

Although the editor makes every effort to verify the accuracy of the information published, BrightSummaries.com accepts no responsibility for the content of this book.

© BrightSummaries.com, 2019. All rights reserved.

www.brightsummaries.com

Ebook EAN: 9782808018937

Paperback EAN: 9782808018944

Legal Deposit: D/2019/12603/113

Cover: © Primento

Digital conception by Primento, the digital partner of publishers.